PUBLIC LIBRARY

W9-AMB-032

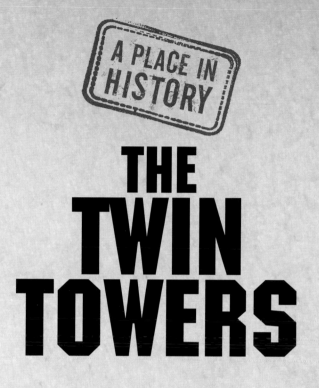

A PLACE IN HISTORY

THE TWIN TOWERS

Sam's father called and told us "you have to get out of there now—those buildings are going to fall." And as soon as we hit the ground, that's when the tower fell. We just saw this huge mushroom cloud coming toward us and then soon enough the cloud overtook us and that's when everything went silent and black.

Quyen Tran, 9/11 survivor

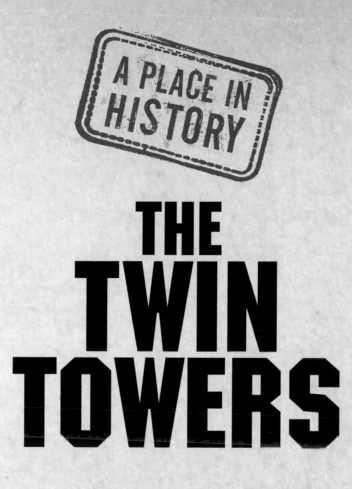

A PLACE IN HISTORY

THE TWIN TOWERS

DAVID ABBOTT

FREMONT PUBLIC LIBRARY DISTRICT
1170 N. Midlothian Road
Mundelein, IL 60060

WITHDRAWN

ARCTURUS

This edition first published in 2010 by Arcturus Publishing
Distributed by Black Rabbit Books
P.O. Box 3263
Mankato
Minnesota MN 56002

Copyright © 2010 Arcturus Publishing Limited

Printed in China

The right of David Abbott to be identified as the author of this work has been asserted by him in accordance with the Copyright, Designs and Patents Act 1988.

All rights reserved.

Series concept: Alex Woolf
Editors: Sean Connolly and Alex Woolf
Designer: Phipps Design
Picture research: Alex Woolf

Library of Congress Cataloging-in-Publication Data

Abbott, David, 1960-
  The Twin Towers / David Abbott.
    p. cm. -- (A place in history)
  Includes bibliographical references and index.
  ISBN 978-1-84837-677-9 (library binding)
  1. September 11 Terrorist Attacks, 2001--Juvenile literature. 2.
World Trade Center (New York, N.Y.)--Juvenile literature. 3.
Terrorism--United States--Juvenile literature. I. Title.
  HV6432.7.A223 2011
  973.931--dc22
              2010014195

Picture credits:
Corbis: cover *background* (Sean Adair/Reuters), cover *foreground* (Shannon Stapleton/Reuters), 6–7 (Bill Ross), 9 (Charles E Rotkin), 15 (Jacques Langevin/Sygma), 16 (Reuters), 17 (Antoine Gyori/Sygma), 18 (Yahya Arhab/ epa), 20 (David Browne/Reuters), 21 (epa), 22 (Jacques Langevin/ Sygma), 23 (Mike Stewart/Sygma), 27 (David Turnley), 28 (Ron Sachs/CNP/Sygma), 29 (Ethan Miller/Reuters), 30 (Robert Patrick), 31 (Reuters), 32 (Filippo Venezia/ epa), 33 (Jim Young/Reuters), 34 (Mike Stewart/Sygma), 36 (Lazim Ali/Reuters), 37 (Steve Raymer), 38 (Peter Turnley), 39 (Brooks Kraft), 40 (Reuters), 41 (Stephen Hird), 42 (Michael Macor/San Francisco Chronicle), 43 (Lower Manhattan Development Corporation/Reuters).
Getty Images: 8 (Frederick Lewis/Hulton Archive), 11 (Time & Life Pictures), 12 (Popperfoto), 13 (Keystone/Hulton Archive), 14 (Gabriel Duval/AFP), 19 (CNN), 26 (Thomas Nilsson), 35 (Bill Pugliano).
Rex Features: 25 (Tamara Beckwith).

Cover pictures:
Background: New York City, September 11, 2001: the South Tower of the World Trade Center bursts into flames after being struck by hijacked United Airlines Flight 175, while the North Tower burns following an earlier attack by another hijacked airliner, American Airlines Flight 11.
Foreground: Rescue workers remove Father Mychal Judge, NYC Fire Department Chaplain, from one of the World Trade Center towers in New York City, September 11, 2001.

Every attempt has been made to clear copyright. Should there be any inadvertent omission, please apply to the publisher for rectification.

SL001443US   Supplier 03 Date 0510

Tomorrow New York is going to be here. And we're going to rebuild, and we're going to be stronger than we were before ... I want the people of New York to be an example to the rest of the country, and the rest of the world, that terrorism can't stop us.

Rudy Giuliani, mayor of New York City at the time of the 9/11 attacks

CONTENTS

1 ONE MORNING IN SEPTEMBER

American Airlines Flight 11 took off from Boston's Logan International Airport at 7:59 a.m. on September 11, 2001, bound for Los Angeles. At 8:13, as the aircraft was passing over central Massachussetts, the stewardesses began serving beverages. Suddenly, five men stood up and began making their way toward the cockpit. Two stewardesses tried to intervene, but the men stabbed them with small knives they'd kept concealed within their clothes. The screams and the sight of blood caused the passengers to start to panic. One jumped up and tried to tackle one of the hijackers, but he was also stabbed. The other passengers could only watch helplessly as the hijackers entered the cockpit…

Boston's air traffic controllers couldn't understand why the pilots were no longer responding. They didn't know yet that the pilots were dead and that Flight 11 was now in the hands of hijackers, one of whom was himself a trained pilot. The hijackers were from an organization called al-Qaeda, an extreme Islamist group. They were not ordinary hijackers. They had no interest in negotiating. They had just one thing on their minds and that was death—on a spectacular scale. The lead hijacker, a man named Mohammed Atta, turned the aircraft sharply to the south and set a new course for New York City. His destination: the Twin Towers.

Until September 11, 2001, the Twin Towers of the World Trade Center, situated at the southern tip of Manhattan Island, dominated the magnificent New York City skyline.

2 THE WORLD TRADE CENTER

ick up any photograph of New York City taken between the early 1970s and 2001 and there they are, the Twin Towers, dominating the Manhattan skyline. Despite the familiarity of the image, few people know how the two towers—part of New York's World Trade Center—came to be built, or what went on inside them.

The idea of the Twin Towers

The idea for a World Trade Center (WTC) in Lower Manhattan was first proposed in 1946, but the plan soon stalled. The man who revived the idea and ensured the towers were built was Austin J. Tobin, executive director of the Port Authority of New York and New Jersey. In the early 1960s Tobin proposed building a giant skyscraper complex in order to provide much needed office space for Lower Manhattan. The plan met considerable opposition at first, both from local residents who did not want to move and from New York City politicians unhappy at their share of the potential tax revenues. Tobin eventually got his way, and Japanese-American architect Minoru Yamasaki was commissioned to design the building. Yamasaki came up with a novel design for a development that included two 110-story twin towers. Once completed in 1971, they were the tallest towers in world, a record they held for two years.

Construction

Yamasaki wanted to provide the maximum amount of floor space in an open floor plan, without supporting columns. To achieve this he used a recently developed tube-frame structural design. The tube frame consisted of steel columns—59 per side—that were placed close to one another to give the towers strong, rigid walls. These, together with the core columns (for elevator and service shafts, toilets, and stairwells) supported the weight of the building. The tube-frame structure had flexibility as well as strength, helping it to withstand high winds.

Japanese-American architect Minoru Yamasaki (1912–86), who designed the World Trade Center.

8

The Twin Towers under construction in February 1971. The towers were officially opened on April 4, 1973. Their construction cost the Port Authority a total of $900 million.

FACT FILE

Vital statistics

- Each tower stood 1,362 feet (410 meters) high and occupied about an acre (4,000 square meters) of land.
- The floors of the Twin Towers were made of four-inch (10-centimeter) thick concrete slabs laid on a steel deck and provided 40,000 square feet (3,716 square meters) of space on each level.
- Each tower provided more than 3.8 million square feet (353,000 square meters) of office space.

Life in the Twin Towers

The huge WTC complex, which in 2001 included five other buildings in addition to the Twin Towers, occupied 16 acres (6.5 hectares) and provided office space for around 50,000 people. It included a hotel, stores, a police station, the highest restaurant in New York, and a train station, as well as offices, trading rooms, and banks.

In its early years the complex struggled to attract the customers from the world of business, and government organizations leased many of the floors. Then, during the 1980s, the financial services industry boomed, and the Twin Towers soon became home to stockbrokers, analysts, banks, and real-estate dealers.

Center of attention

Not everyone thought the Twin Towers were pleasant to look at or work in. Nevertheless the towers soon became an iconic feature of the New York skyline, as well known as the Empire State Building and the Chrysler Building. The Top of the World observation deck in the South Tower and the Windows

Philippe Petit begins his high-wire walk on August 7, 1974. He posed as a construction worker to gain access to the South Tower roof.

on the World restaurant in the North Tower were major tourist destinations.

Their dizzying height soon attracted daredevils. Early one morning in the summer of 1974, a French high-wire artist, Philippe Petit, rigged up a steel cable between the

FACT FILE

High and mighty

It has been estimated that between 140,000 and 200,000 people worked in or visited the WTC each day. The towers were home to between 400 and 500 businesses. Famous names such as Fuji Bank, Cantor Fitzgerald, Morgan Stanley, Hyundai, and MetLife all set up offices there.

10

two towers. Petit walked back and forth between the towers and sat and lay on the wire, at a height of 1,345 feet (410 meters). After a display of 45 minutes, Petit came off the wire and was arrested by the police. Three years later a Brooklyn toymaker, George Willig, also known as "the human fly," scaled the South Tower.

The Twin Towers were also attracting the attention of less benign individuals. In February 1993—foreshadowing a far more terrible event eight-and-a-half years later—the towers were attacked by al-Qaeda. The terrorists exploded a one-ton car bomb in the public parking area beneath the WTC. The attackers hoped the bomb would cause the towers to collapse. They failed in this, but six people died and more than a thousand were injured by the explosion.

VOICES

Decadence or zest?

For its destroyers, the Twin Towers were a symbol of greed and decadence. Others saw it differently. Martin Amis, the British writer, said: *The World Trade Center was a symbol of indigenous mobility and zest, and of the galaxy of glittering destinations.*
Minoru Yamasaki, chief architect of the WTC, said: *The World Trade Center is a living symbol of man's dedication to world peace.*

Following the 1993 bombing of the WTC, a rescue worker searches for injured people among debris in the underground parking area.

3. THE RISE OF ISLAMISM

What motivated the terrorists who attacked the Twin Towers on September 11, 2001? The roots of the event can be traced to a time almost a century earlier, thousands of miles from New York, in the Middle East, where a movement arose that came to be known as Islamism.

In this early 20th-century photo, wealthy British colonists are attended by Egyptian horsemen. Britain's occupation of Egypt, which began in 1882, stirred up a great deal of popular resentment.

The decline of the Ottoman Empire

In the early 20th century the region that we call the Middle East (southwestern Asia and northeastern Africa) was a part of the Ottoman Empire. The people of this empire were mostly Arabs and overwhelmingly Muslim. The empire, by this time, was in a state of terminal decline. European powers

FACT FILE

The Ottoman Empire

The Ottoman Empire lasted from 1299 until 1923. At its peak, from its capital in Constantinople (now called Istanbul), it controlled territory in Europe, Asia, and North Africa.

had begun to dominate many of its provinces. They introduced modern Western goods and Western-style institutions, including law courts, banks, and schools.

Local rulers within the empire welcomed this process of Westernization, but it also caused anger and resentment among devout Muslims. They formed the Islamic Movement in an effort to revive a stricter form of Islam. The Islamic Movement was anti-modern and anti-Western. It pushed for the reintroduction of Sharia—Islamic holy law.

The Ottoman Empire finally collapsed following its defeat in World War I. Some parts of the empire, like Palestine, Iraq, and Lebanon, fell under the rule of France and Britain; others, such as Turkey, Egypt, and Iran, grew into nations with moderate, Western-supporting leaders.

Sayyid Qutb

During this period, various groups formed to oppose Western dominance and preach a return to strict Islamic values. The most influential of these was the Muslim Brotherhood, founded in Egypt in 1928 by Hasan al-Banna. The Brotherhood quickly spread throughout the Muslim world. One of its leading thinkers was Sayyid Qutb (1906–66). He believed it was the duty of Muslims to engage in violent struggle—jihad—against the enemies of Islam. His writings would influence radical Muslims for years to come, among them the young Osama bin Laden. Qutb was, in this sense, probably the true founder of Islamism.

Israel, Palestine, and Iran

In 1948 the Jewish state of Israel was established in the former British territory of Palestine, causing the exodus of hundreds of thousands of Palestinian Arabs to surrounding Arab states. This aroused the hostility of the Arab Muslim world, some members of which set out to destroy Israel.

A Palestinian woman arrives with her child in Port Said, Egypt, in May 1948, seeking refuge from the conflict with Israel. Some 750,000 Palestinians fled their homeland during the war.

VOICES

We won't be you

Samuel Huntingdon, Professor of Government at Harvard University, described the revival of Islam as follows: *... the revival of Islam is a rejection of the West. It is a declaration of cultural independence from the West, a proud statement that: "We will be modern but we won't be you."*

The Clash of Civilizations by Samuel P. Huntingdon (Simon & Schuster, 1998)

13

Ayatollah Ruhollah Khomeini, the founder of Iran's Islamic republic, waves to supporters in Tehran following the revolution in February 1979. Khomeini, a religious leader, had returned after 15 years in exile.

FACT FILE

The Iranian Revolution

In the late 1970s the shah (ruler) of Iran lost support from all sections of Iranian society, due to the unpopularity of his economic policies, his brutal secret police, and because he was seen as an "American puppet." Civil unrest forced the shah into exile in January 1979, and in April a new constitution established Iran as an Islamic republic. A senior Shia cleric, Ayatollah Khomeini, was installed as supreme leader.

The Jewish state survived and prospered, however, with Western, especially American, help. Many in the Muslim world took up the cause of Palestinian liberation. Some people resorted to terrorist violence against Israeli and Western targets.

In 1979 the Islamists scored a major victory with the establishment, in Iran, of the first modern Islamist state. Iran was not an Arab country and it followed Shia Islam, the minority branch of the religion. Nevertheless, the Iranian Revolution had a major impact, inspiring Islamist movements throughout the Muslim world.

Anti-Americanism

Islamism has many roots, including the failure of post-independence Arab governments to deliver prosperity, the writings of Sayyid Qutb, and the Palestinian issue. Another major cause is anti-Americanism. As the leading Western power, the United States exercises great influence over the Middle East in its ability to persuade Muslim governments to act in its interests. American culture, in the form of food brands, movies, television, music, and fashion, also has a strong impact. Islamists view this culture as decadent. American foreign policy is also very unpopular, particularly its consistent support for Israel and its military interventions in the Muslim countries of Iraq and Afghanistan. The United States has thus come to be seen by Islamists as corrupt, decadent, and aggressive—an example of all that is wrong with the West.

The stationing of US troops in the Muslim holy land of Saudi Arabia during the Persian Gulf War (1991) greatly angered the Saudi-born Islamist Osama bin Laden. It was this that prompted him to turn toward terrorism. In 1993 US troops intervened in Mogadishu in Muslim Somalia,

> ### VOICES
>
> ### *We are the victims of terrorism*
>
> In an interview given to ABC News in 1998, Osama bin Laden, the al-Qaeda leader, explained why he saw America as the enemy of all Muslim people:
>
> *The truth is that the whole Muslim world is the victim of international terrorism, engineered by America at the United Nations. We are a nation whose sacred symbols have been looted and whose wealth and resources have been plundered.*
>
> ABC News at www.pbs.org

trying to restore order as warring ethnic groups attempted to gain power. Islamists celebrated when the Somali militia defeated the Americans, causing many casualties. This demonstrated that the United States was not invincible.

US troops on patrol in the Arabian Desert in Saudi Arabia during the Persian Gulf War of 1991. Their presence there outraged Osama bin Laden.

A clash of civilizations?

The influential US scholar Samuel Huntingdon (1927–2008) argued in 1996 that, in the future, the main cause of world conflict would be to do with culture and religion, rather than ideas. Muslims, for example, would increasingly see themselves as a separate civilization in conflict with the culture and values of Western civilization. Huntingdon warned that the West would lose its power and influence if it did not understand this. At the time, Huntingdon's views were seen as controversial, but after the attacks in the United States on September 11, 2001, they seemed prophetic.

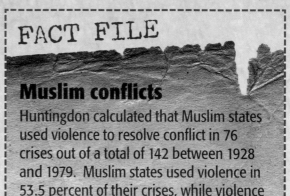

FACT FILE

Muslim conflicts

Huntingdon calculated that Muslim states used violence to resolve conflict in 76 crises out of a total of 142 between 1928 and 1979. Muslim states used violence in 53.5 percent of their crises, while violence was used by the UK in 11.5 percent of cases, by the United States in 17.9 percent and by the Soviet Union in 28.5 percent of cases.

Source: *The Clash of Civilizations* by Samuel P. Huntingdon (Simon & Schuster, 1998)

Samuel Huntington predicted that future world conflicts would be between cultures rather than states. He identified seven or eight competing cultures, including the West and Islam, and suggested that the West would need to strengthen its own culture in order to survive.

Demolishing myths

Critics of Huntingdon's analysis, such as Professor Fred Halliday of the London School of Economics, point out that Islamic societies are deeply divided. For example, the bloodiest Middle Eastern war of recent decades was the Iran–Iraq War (1980–88) between two Muslim states. Many of the world's Muslim states are on friendly terms with the West. Halliday argues that the current tensions in Muslim states are more often than not about attempts by anti-Western Islamists to gain control of pro-Western regimes.

Halliday also sees little sign of cultural battle lines being drawn up within Western

Islamists burn a flag in Peshawar, Pakistan. Scenes such as this seem to give support to the "clash of civilizations" theory. However, it only tells part of the story: in Pakistan, many Muslims do not support the Islamists.

societies. He claims that the term "Islamophobia" was created by radical Muslim groups living in the West in the 1990s, but that Western societies are not, in fact, generally hostile to Islam. Contemporary prejudices, says Halliday, are against Muslims as people, rather than against Islam as a religion or culture. So while Islamists and some Western commentators like to portray a world divided by cultural values and beliefs, the reality is much more complicated.

VOICES

Two views

Compare the views of academics Samuel Huntingdon and Fred Halliday. Huntingdon argues that: *Wherever one looks along the perimeter of Islam, Muslims have problems living peaceably with their neighbors.* However, Halliday counters: *The history of Europe in the twentieth century, and the brutality visited by some of its rulers on their own peoples, far outstrips anything seen in the modern Middle East.*

From *The Clash of Civilizations* by Samuel P. Huntingdon (Simon & Schuster, 1998) and *100 Myths about the Middle East* by Fred Halliday (Saqi, 2005)

4 AL-QAEDA

The men who hijacked the planes on September 11, 2001, were part of a terrorist group called al-Qaeda. The group was founded in Pakistan in 1988 by the Saudi-born millionaire Osama bin Laden and his Islamist mentor, Abdullah Azzam (see page 20).

Structure

No one apart from those involved know for sure how al-Qaeda is structured. According to the testimony of one former member, Jamal al-Fadl, it has a core membership of 20 to 30 people, who deal with matters such as military operations, finance, Islamic law, and the media. However, other experts dispute that al-Qaeda even exists as a formal organization. They describe it as a network of separate terrorist groups based in different parts of the world, which share a common ideology (set of beliefs).

Membership

Al-Qaeda members are Sunni Muslims who want to see the creation of a new caliphate—a united Islamic empire. In the early years of al-Qaeda's existence, members were mainly Arabs. For example, the terrorists who attacked the United States on September 11, 2001, were mainly from Saudi Arabia and the Gulf states. In recent years Pakistanis have been the predominant nationality. Contrary

Al-Qaeda militants on trial in Yemen in 2009. Terrorist organizations thrive in places like Yemen where government control is weak. Yemen has become a key center of recruitment for al-Qaeda.

FACT FILE

Educated militants

Around 63 percent of al-Qaeda members have university degrees. Mohammed Atta, who took part in the September 11 attacks, had a PhD in City Planning. The terrorists involved in a 2007 attack on Glasgow Airport in the UK were medical doctors.

Source for statistic: *Understanding Terror Networks* by Dr. Marc Sageman (University of Pennsylvania Press, 2004)

This image, taken from a collection of videotapes obtained by CNN, shows suspected members of al-Qaeda celebrating after a training exercise.

to popular belief, those who join al-Qaeda are not all desperately poor; many operatives are well educated and have university degrees. US foreign policy expert Dr. Marc Sageman says they are often from middle-class families and may not even be particularly religious to begin with. The bonds of family and friendship are a more common reason for young Muslims to join the jihad.

Who is Osama bin Laden?

Osama bin Laden was born in 1957 in Riyadh, Saudi Arabia. His father, Mohammed, migrated to Saudi Arabia from Yemen and began work as a porter. Mohammed became tremendously wealthy after starting up a construction company. He married eleven women and had 54 children. Osama was his seventeenth son. When Osama was ten, his father died in an air accident. He was then brought up by his mother and stepfather in Jeddah. In the 1970s he attended King Abdul Aziz University in Jeddah, though it is unclear whether he graduated. Various sources describe him as studying either public administration or engineering.

VOICES

Declaring jihad

We declared jihad against the US government, because the US government is unjust, criminal, and tyrannical. It has committed acts that are extremely unjust, hideous, and criminal, whether directly or through its support of the Israeli occupation of Palestine. And we believe the US is directly responsible for those who were killed in Palestine, Lebanon, and Iraq.

Osama bin Laden, CNN interview, 1997

Politics and religion

At university, bin Laden is thought to have fallen under the influence of Abdullah Azzam, a radical Islamist scholar. Azzam introduced bin Laden to the writings of Sayyid Qutb. Bin Laden came to believe in the restoration of the Caliphate under Sharia law. He blamed the downfall of the previous Caliphate (the Ottoman Empire) on the decadence and pro-Western policies of its leaders. He saw similar corruption and Western influence in the regimes that ruled much of the contemporary Muslim world and believed that only jihad (violent struggle) could restore strict Islamic rule.

Afghanistan

Abdullah Azzam recruited bin Laden to join the Afghan mujahidin (Arabic for "freedom fighters") in their fight to repel the Soviet invasion of their country (1979–89). He and Azzam formed Maktab al-Khidamat (MAK), a support organization for the mujahidin. Bin Laden used his wealth to provide funds, training, weapons, and equipment for the mujahidin. He is also thought to have taken an active role in some of the fighting.

When the Soviet Union withdrew from Afghanistan in 1989, bin Laden and Azzam decided to use the contacts they had made through MAK to wage a broader jihad against those they saw as "enemies of Islam." They formed a new organization called al-Qaeda, which means simply "the Base" or "the Foundation." This name reflected al-Qaeda's strategy: to form a base from which a large

FACT FILE

Family life

Osama bin Laden married his first wife in 1974, at 17. According to some sources, he had married four women by 2002 and fathered between 12 and 26 children.

Afghan mujahidin fire at enemy aircraft during the war against the Soviet Union (1979–89).

Osama bin Laden in a cave in the Jalalabad region of Afghanistan in 1988. Following the defeat of the Soviet Union, his thoughts turned to global jihad.

network of groups, committed to jihad, could be set up all over the world. When Azzam was killed in 1989, bin Laden became the sole leader of the emerging organization.

Sudan

Through his father, bin Laden had close links with the Saudi royal family. But on his return from Afghanistan, he fell out with the Saudi government over its willingness to allow US military bases on its territory. In 1992 bin Laden found a new base for al-Qaeda in Sudan. The country was ruled by the Islamist National Islamic Front, whose leader, Hassan al-Turabi, was a great admirer of bin Laden.

VOICES

Justified terrorism?

Every state and every civilization and culture has to resort to terrorism under certain circumstances for the purpose of abolishing tyranny and corruption. The terrorism we practice is of the commendable kind for it is directed at the tyrants and the aggressors and the enemies of Allah, the tyrants, the traitors who commit acts of treason against their own countries and their own faith and their own prophet and their own nation.

Osama bin Laden, in an interview with John Miller of ABC News, 1998

Girls study on a terrace roof in Afghanistan following the overthrow of the Taliban in November 2001. Under the Taliban, a few schools carried on teaching girls in secret, at great risk to their teachers and parents.

FACT FILE

The Taliban

The Taliban is an extreme Islamist group that ruled Afghanistan from 1995 to 2001. Its leaders followed a strict interpretation of Sharia law and aimed to create the world's purest Islamic state. They banned all "corrupting influences" such as television, music, and movies. Women were denied education or the right to work and were forced to cover themselves from head to foot in a garment called a burka. Adultery was punishable by stoning, and the hands and feet of thieves were amputated. Those who did not pray five times a day or fast (abstain from food) during the Muslim holy month of Ramadan were imprisoned.

Establishing alliances

Bin Laden spent the next few years building up a network of alliances with militant Islamist groups throughout the Middle East, North Africa, southern Asia and Europe. As well as sending financial and military assistance to jihadis in Algeria, Egypt, and Afghanistan, al-Qaeda also targeted the United States for its continued siting of military bases in the holy land of Saudi Arabia. They were responsible for, or assisted in, a string of terrorist attacks, including bomb attacks in Aden, Yemen, in 1992 and the 1993 World Trade Center bombing.

In 1996 Sudan bowed to international pressure and was forced to eject al-Qaeda. Bin Laden took his organization to Afghanistan, which was by then ruled by an Islamist group, the Taliban. Bin Laden made

The damaged destroyer, USS *Cole*, in Aden, Yemen. Al-Qaeda terrorists sailed a boat alongside the ship and detonated explosives, tearing a large hole in the vessel's port side.

an alliance with the Taliban, which enabled al-Qaeda to establish a secure base there from which to continue its global jihad.

Declaration of war

In August 1996 bin Laden issued a fatwa (religious ruling) entitled "The Declaration of War." In it he warned the United States to withdraw its military presence from Saudi Arabia or action would be taken against it. Another fatwa in February 1998 called on Muslims to kill Americans and their allies. The following August, hundreds were killed in simultaneous bomb attacks on the US embassies in Tanzania and Kenya. In October 2000 al-Qaeda terrorists launched a suicide attack on the US naval vessel USS *Cole* in Yemen, killing 17 sailors. For those who cared to read them, the signs were clear that a big attack was about to be launched.

VOICES

A duty to kill

In 1998 Osama bin Laden issued the following fatwa in the name of the World Islamic Front for Jihad against Jews and Crusaders:

The ruling to kill the Americans and their allies—civilians and military— is an individual duty for every Muslim who can do it in any country in which it is possible to do it, in order to liberate the al-Aqsa Mosque [in Jerusalem] and the holy mosque [in Mecca] from their grip, and in order for their armies to move out of all the lands of Islam, defeated and unable to threaten any Muslim.

5. THE ATTACK

In New York City, Tuesday September 11, 2001, began as a beautiful sunny morning. As the morning rush hour reached its peak, the streets and sidewalks were full of people hurrying to work in the financial district. The Twin Towers of the World Trade Center, standing clear above all the other high-rise buildings in Lower Manhattan, glittered in the late summer sunshine, the morning sun reflecting in their windows.

Flight 11

At 8:46 a.m. American Airlines Flight 11, which had been commandeered by Mohammed Atta and his fellow hijackers, appeared low in the sky above Manhattan. Flying at around 450 mph (750 km/h), the aircraft slammed into the North Tower of the World Trade Center between the 93rd and 99th floors. There was a huge explosion as around 10,000 gallons of jet fuel, needed for the intended journey to Los Angeles, ignited. All the passengers, including the hijackers, died instantly. Hundreds working in the tower were killed by the impact. The blast made the tower sway from side to side and survivors reported they heard loud grinding noises as the bolts on the exterior walls were put under extreme tension.

Flight 175

Seventeen minutes later, while New Yorkers were still trying to come to terms with what had just happened, United Airlines Flight 175 began its approach from the southwest. The aircraft was under the control of five al-Qaeda terrorists, led by Marwan al-Shehhi. At 9:03 a.m. al-Shehhi flew the second plane into the South Tower. All 65 passengers on board died instantly, as did hundreds more inside the building. The sky was filled with debris: paper blown out from the building and a thick cloud of smoke from the fire.

FACT FILE

A coordinated attack

The attacks on the Twin Towers were only part of al-Qaeda's plans for that morning. Two other planes were also hijacked. At 9:37 a.m. American Airlines Flight 77 flew into the Pentagon, headquarters of the Department of Defense in Arlington, Virginia; at 10:02 a.m. United Airlines Flight 93 crashed into a field in Pennsylvania as passengers attempted to overpower the hijackers. Flight 93 may have been heading for the White House or the United States Capitol, where Congress was in session. The intention was clear: the attack would be a shocking blow against the symbols of America's economic, military, and political power.

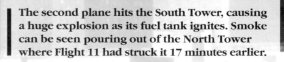

The second plane hits the South Tower, causing a huge explosion as its fuel tank ignites. Smoke can be seen pouring out of the North Tower where Flight 11 had struck it 17 minutes earlier.

In the North Tower, 1,344 people working on the floors above the crash sites were trapped, because all stairwells and elevators around the impact zones had been rendered impassable. In the South Tower, 700 workers found themselves in the same situation.

Many of those trapped managed to phone relatives and friends—it was the last time they would speak to their loved ones. They died from fire or smoke inhalation, from jumping or falling from the buildings, or in the buildings' eventual collapse.

ineffective, so communication was difficult. The failure of the sprinkler system and the fire's sheer intensity made extinguishing it impossible; rescuing those inside was the only option. Many firefighters arriving from outside the area were unfamiliar with the buildings. In addition, falling debris—

> Although the South Tower was the second to be hit, it was the first to collapse. This was because of the sharper angle of impact.

The towers collapse

In the North Tower, the impact of the aircraft demolished about 35 exterior girders. In the South Tower, the impact of Flight 175 destroyed four floors. Experts say that the towers had been designed to withstand much greater forces from hurricane winds. What led the towers to collapse were the intense fires that burned within them, weakening the steel trusses and girders.

The fires caused the floors to sag, pulling the perimeter columns inward so they could no longer support the mass of the building above. The South Tower collapsed at 9:59 a.m. and the North Tower at 10:28 a.m. About 2,750 people were killed in the attack on the Twin Towers, including 345 firefighters and 60 police officers.

Search and rescue

Fire units arrived quickly at the scene but their rescue efforts were hampered by the ferocious blaze inside the towers. The signal amplifier system in the tower had been destroyed, making the firefighters' radios

VOICES

Rescue mission

We had a large volume of fire on the upper floors. Each floor was approximately an acre in size. Several floors of fire would have been beyond the fire-extinguishing capability of the forces we had on hand. So we determined, very early on, that this was going to be strictly a rescue mission.

Fire chief Peter Hayward, commenting on the situation at the North Tower including people jumping from the towers—made it dangerous just moving around outside and getting people to safety.

Ground Zero

After the collapse of both towers, emergency workers, firefighters, and medics all helped in attempts to rescue people. One day after the disaster, rescuers pulled 11 people from the rubble. Such was the devastation that the scene was described as "Ground Zero" by one journalist. First used in 1945 to describe the point on the ground above which the first atomic bombs were exploded over Japan, the term seemed appropriate again, and the name stuck.

Firefighters sift through the wreckage of the Twin Towers. Due to radio communication problems, many firefighters did not hear the order to evacuate. As a result, hundreds were killed or injured when the towers collapsed.

FACT FILE

Toxic dust

The clouds of dust and debris caused by the collapse of the Twin Towers were highly toxic, containing lead and dioxin from the burning jet fuel, mercury from fluorescent lights and cadmium from computers, as well as asbestos and PCBs. Several deaths have been linked to the dust, and the term "Ground Zero illness" has been coined to describe ailments associated with the disaster.

Aftermath

The attacks took everyone—including the US government—completely by surprise. No one in authority had ever dreamed that terrorists would hijack airplanes and turn them into flying bombs. The event quickly became abbreviated to 9/11—an ominous echo of the emergency telephone number.

The Central Intelligence Agency (CIA) and Federal Bureau of Investigation (FBI)—the main intelligence agencies of the United States—were set to work to find out who was responsible. They soon found material indicating links to al-Qaeda, including some of Mohammed Atta's luggage, which had been left at the airport in Boston.

President George W. Bush, who was visiting a school in Florida when he was told of the attacks, was ushered to safety by his secret service staff. He returned to Washington later in the day and spoke to the American people on television, praising the rescuers, commemorating the dead and promising to punish those responsible.

A 21st-century Pearl Harbor?

The attacks of 9/11 were deeply shocking to the American people and the world at large. It was the largest and bloodiest terrorist operation in history and its victims included citizens of more than 90 countries. Police officers and rescue workers from other US cities traveled to New York to assist in the recovery of bodies at Ground Zero. Blood donations across the country soared.

President Bush is said to have to written in his diary that night that the world had witnessed the "Pearl Harbor of the 21st century." He was evoking comparisons with the Japanese attack on the US fleet in 1941—the last time the country had suffered such a sudden and devastating assault on its homeland.

European heads of state sent messages of condolence to President Bush. In London the US national anthem was played at the Changing of the Guard ceremony, and in Berlin thousands of people joined a march to demonstrate their

---

FACT FILE

Flights grounded

The US Federal Aviation Authority (FAA) grounded all aircraft at 9:42 a.m. and all incoming flights to the United States were diverted to airports in Canada, leaving thousands of passengers stranded. For the first time ever, all international passenger flights to and from the United States were banned. The ban lasted for three days.

President Bush broadcasts to the nation from the White House on the evening of 9/11. "None of us will ever forget this day," he said.

condemnation of the attacks. There were also denunciations from Muslim countries, but residents in some of the Palestinian refugee camps celebrated in the streets, and Saddam Hussein, president of Iraq, said that the Americans had only themselves to blame.

A young girl waves an American flag as she sits on her father's shoulders during a candlelight vigil in Las Vegas, held to honor those killed in the terrorist attacks of 9/11.

VOICES

Terrorism can't stop us

Rudy Giuliani, mayor of New York City, was widely praised for his leadership following the attacks. He coordinated the response of the city's emergency departments, helped to direct the search and rescue efforts, and made frequent morale-boosting public statements. He said:

Tomorrow New York is going to be here. And we're going to rebuild, and we're going to be stronger than we were before … I want the people of New York to be an example to the rest of the country, and the rest of the world, that terrorism can't stop us.

6. AMERICA FIGHTS BACK

Once Osama bin Laden and al-Qaeda had been identified as the perpetrators of 9/11, President Bush's administration was quick to roll out a plan of action. Al-Qaeda was based in Taliban-controlled Afghanistan and it was in this direction that the eyes of the world now turned. On September 20, Bush addressed both houses of Congress in a speech that was broadcast to the nation. He demanded that the Taliban hand over bin Laden and the other al-Qaeda leaders to US authorities and that they close all al-Qaeda training camps in Afghanistan.

Northern Alliance soldiers observe US airstrikes against Taliban forces during Operation Enduring Freedom. The Northern Alliance consisted of several ethnic groups and religious factions.

Operation Enduring Freedom

The Taliban rejected President Bush's ultimatum and, on October 7, 2001, the United States launched Operation Enduring Freedom. A US-led coalition began bombing Taliban and al-Qaeda training camps and bases in Afghanistan. Coalition forces used a combination of air power and small numbers of special forces working closely with the Taliban's Afghan opponents, the Northern Alliance, to fight the Taliban.

VOICES

War on Terror

The phrase "War on Terror" was first used by President Bush in his September 20, 2001, speech to Congress:
Our war on terror begins with al-Qaeda, but it does not end there. It will not end until every terrorist group of global reach has been found, stopped, and defeated.
The phrase has become associated with the style and policies of the Bush administration. It has not been used by his successor President Barack Obama. In March 2009 the US Defense Department changed the name from "Global War on Terror" to "Overseas Contingency Operation."

This proved to be an effective strategy in the short term. The capital Kabul was captured on November 13. The Taliban were driven back into the southeast of the country and the mountainous borderlands with Pakistan. Some Taliban forces, possibly including bin Laden, retreated to an area called Tora Bora, close to the Pakistan border. Coalition forces soon overran al-Qaeda and Taliban positions at Tora Bora, but bin Laden was not found. The Taliban had been overthrown, and al-Qaeda had been driven from its Afghan bases, but neither had been destroyed, and they would soon recommence their attacks.

May 2002: Coalition forces in the Tora Bora region prepare explosives to blow up a network of bunkers and caves being used by al-Qaeda and Taliban fighters.

FACT FILE

The Bush Doctrine

President Bush took the view that it was legitimate for the United States to defend itself by launching preemptive attacks against foreign regimes that presented a potential threat to US national security. That included both hostile regimes and regimes that harbored terrorists. Bush's views were explained in a document entitled National Security Strategy of the United States, published in September 2002, and which subsequently became known as the Bush Doctrine. The doctrine was used to justify the invasions of Afghanistan (2001) and Iraq (2003).

FACT FILE

Economic cost

9/11 had economic as well as political and military consequences. The New York Stock Exchange closed for the rest of the week, insurance losses were estimated at around $40 billion and one analyst from the Fiscal Policy Institute in New York estimated that the attack was directly responsible for the loss of around 79,300 jobs.

Police stand guard in front of a money transfer agency in Brescia, Italy, which was being used to fund an Islamist terrorist group in Pakistan.

Terrorist finances

International terrorists need access to large sums of cash; in the build up to 9/11, for example, the terrorists had to pay for expensive flying lessons, rent accommodation, and purchase business-class air tickets. The Bush administration therefore put considerable effort into actions that would cut off terrorist financing and make it harder for them to plan and launch attacks.

A new law, the USA PATRIOT Act, was passed by Congress soon after 9/11, allowing the government to monitor communications between suspected terrorists and carry out searches to help uncover terrorist plots. The USA PATRIOT Act also included new rules to prevent money laundering: Banks were required to keep records and routinely investigate large transfers of money.

International action

The US government was not alone in taking tough action against terrorism. Many countries, including the United Kingdom, France, Russia, Germany, India, Pakistan, and China introduced anti-terrorism legislation to freeze bank accounts of organizations and individuals suspected of having al-Qaeda links.

To defeat a global terrorist network, coordinated international efforts were also necessary. By 2003 the United Nations (UN) had adopted 12 conventions and protocols to combat terrorism. These required states to, for example, take steps to increase the security of aircraft and nuclear facilities, as well as freeze the assets of terrorist networks. The UN published a list of 293 individuals and groups whose assets should be frozen by member nations.

Lapses in security

The US government also had to ask searching questions about how the attacks had been been allowed to occur. Why had security procedures failed and how could they be strengthened in future? This was one of the key questions that the 9/11 Commission, established in November 2002, set out to answer.

The commission concluded that blind spots existed in security at all levels, from airport security personnel to the way that the CIA and FBI collected and shared information. In the phrase of one expert testifying to the 9/11 Commission, in the summer of 2001, "the system was blinking red," but vital clues indicating that a big attack was imminent were not acted upon.

The chairman of the 9/11 Commission Thomas Kean (left) and Vice Chairman Lee Hamilton. Kean said that 9/11 could have been prevented if the US government had taken preemptive action against al-Qaeda and acted on intelligence it had been given.

VOICES

Missed chances

The 9/11 Commission identified numerous occasions where vital intelligence was not shared by US government agencies:

In the 9/11 story ... we sometimes see examples of information that could be accessed—like the undistributed NSA [National Security Agency] information that would have helped identify Nawaz al-Hamzi [one of the organizers of 9/11] in January 2000. But someone had to ask for it. In that case, no one did.

9/11 Commission Report, p.417

Security cameras at Portland Airport, Maine, captured this image of Mohammed Atta (right) and an accomplice going through security before flying to Boston on the morning of 9/11.

On 9/11 several of the terrorists were stopped by airport security staff when the CAPPS (Computer Assisted Passenger Prescreening System) security equipment indicated a problem. Two of the terrorists boarding Flight 77 set off metal detector alarms, but nothing was found and they were allowed to board the airplane.

Among the 9/11 Commission's recommendations, it suggested that the government should:

- use intelligence about terrorist funding to track down cells and disrupt their operations;
- exchange information with trusted allies
- improve border security and the screening of travelers;
- improve intelligence gathering and interagency cooperation.

Security at airports did improve significantly after 9/11. New procedures included more checks, an insistence on sufficient identification and a ban on the carrying of sharp objects in hand luggage—the 9/11 terrorists had used box cutters or Stanley knives, which have short but very sharp blades.

In 2002 a new US government department was created, the Department of Homeland Security. This was intended to join up key services, such as immigration, customs,

FACT FILE

British anti-terror laws

The British Parliament passed a series of anti-terrorism laws in the years after 9/11. This legislation included provisions for:

- foreign terrorist suspects to be detained indefinitely;
- terrorist suspects to be detained without charge for up to 28 days;
- the introduction of control orders— a form of house arrest for terrorist suspects.

border control, and citizenship services (the provision of passports), to avoid the communication failures that had contributed to 9/11.

Security and civil liberties

The USA PATRIOT Act of 2001 gave US security services much greater powers to search for terrorists. The FBI, for example, was given the power to search telephone, bank, and email records without having to apply for permission from a court. The act also made it easier for the security services to tap telephones, cell phones, or computers and to obtain a search warrant in suspected terrorist cases. Opponents of the law saw it as an erosion of the civil liberties of US citizens. They have criticized its provisions that immigrants suspected of being terrorists can be held indefinitely without charge and that people's homes can be searched without their permission, or have their phones tapped without a court order.

VOICES

Not America

Senator Russ Feingold made the following statement during the debate on the USA PATRIOT Act:

Of course, there is no doubt that if we lived in a police state, it would be easier to catch terrorists … But that probably would not be a country in which we would want to live. And that would not be a country for which we could, in good conscience, ask our young people to fight and die. In short, that would not be America.

US Senator Russ Feingold, October 3, 2001

Not all Americans agreed with the measures taken to improve security. Protesters in Detroit express their opposition to John Ashcroft, the US Attorney General at the time and a keen upholder of the USA PATRIOT Act.

7. THE WIDENING WAR

The War on Terror, which began with the invasion of Afghanistan, soon widened as the United States provided military assistance to other countries fighting al-Qaeda terrorist cells. These included Georgia, Kyrgyzstan, Uzbekistan, and the Philippines. However, the Bush administration's next major target in the war would be Iraq.

Many in the Bush administration were convinced that the Iraqi dictator Saddam Hussein had played a role in the 9/11 attacks. According to senior policy official Stephen Cambone, as early as 2:40 p.m. on September 11, Secretary of Defense Donald Rumsfeld asked his aides to look for evidence of Iraqi involvement.

Iraq and the United States

President Bush and several key figures in his administration took the view that an attack like 9/11 was too complex to have been carried out by a

FACT FILE

Axis of evil

On January 29, 2002, President Bush made his annual State of the Union address to Congress. He said that "Iraq is a regime that has something to hide from the civilized world." Speaking of Iraq, Iran and North Korea, he went on to say that "states like these, and their terrorist allies, constitute an axis of evil, aiming to threaten the peace of the world."

Iraqi leader Saddam Hussein liked to portray himself as a tough leader, prepared to stand up to America.

The Iraq War ignited worldwide protests. While most agreed that Hussein was a brutal dictator, not everyone viewed Iraq as a threat to world peace.

group without the support of a foreign state. The United States had developed a deep distrust of Hussein since his invasion of Kuwait, which sparked the Gulf War of 1990–91. Since 1998 US foreign policy had formally expressed a desire that Iraq be liberated from Hussein's rule.

In fact, no links were found between the Hussein regime and al-Qaeda. However, the Bush administration remained concerned that Hussein might be developing weapons of mass destruction (WMD)—nuclear, biological, or chemical weapons. They feared that he might share these WMD with terrorist groups. For this reason, removing Hussein was viewed as part of the War on Terror.

Invasion

UN weapons inspectors failed to find evidence of WMD in Iraq. Despite this, in March 2003, a US-led coalition invaded Iraq.

VOICES

A better place

The official reason for the invasion of Iraq was Hussein's development of WMD. But WMD were never found. British Prime Minister Tony Blair said in 2004:

I can apologise for the information that turned out to be wrong, but I can't, sincerely at least, apologise for removing Saddam. The world is a better place with Saddam in prison not in power.

From a speech to the Labour Party Conference, September 28, 2004

The Iraq War marked the first serious division among coalition partners in the War on Terror, with several countries, including France, Russia, and China, opposing the invasion. They saw it as a distraction from the real war against al-Qaeda and were not convinced that Hussein posed a major threat to global security. There were also significant popular protests against the war in many countries.

37

A dictator toppled: many Iraqis celebrated the downfall of Saddam Hussein by destroying or vandalizing portraits and statues of him.

Hussein's regime was overthrown within weeks. However, the occupation by Coalition forces sparked a major insurgency. Pro-Hussein Sunni militias, Iranian-backed Shia groups, and al-Qaeda fighters from abroad, attacked Coalition forces and one other, making much of Iraq ungovernable and subject to almost daily terrorist attacks. Order was finally restored in most of the country by 2009. By this time an Iraqi government and military had been established and Coalition forces could start to withdraw.

Guantánamo Bay

The Bush administration described al-Qaeda fighters captured in Afghanistan and other conflict zones as "unlawful combatants" or "battlefield detainees" rather than prisoners of war (POWs). In this way, they avoided having to treat them in accordance with the Geneva Conventions, a set of international agreements that protect the rights of POWs. From 2002, detainees were imprisoned at Guantánamo Bay Detention Camp in Cuba, where they would not be subject to US legal jurisdiction.

Some of those held at the camp claimed they had been tortured. One torture was "waterboarding"— pouring water over a prisoner's face to induce a feeling of drowning. Others alleged they had been tortured with broken glass, barbed wire, and burning cigarettes. A 2007 FBI report detailed other forms of torture carried out at the detention camp. These included being chained hand and foot in a fetal position for 18 hours or more and being subjected to extremes of heat and cold. Pictures of prisoners clad in bright orange uniforms and penned into cramped, wire-fenced compounds were transmitted all around the world. In January 2009 President Obama announced that Guantánamo Bay Detention Camp would be closed.

Abu Ghraib

In 2004 American journalists revealed that Iraqi prisoners in Abu Ghraib, near Baghdad, Iraq, had been subjected to physical, psychological, and sexual abuse, including torture and rape, by their American guards. Photographs proving the abuse were published in newspapers and on the internet. A number of US servicemen and women were court-martialed and found guilty. It was subsequently found that service personnel had also abused prisoners at Bagram Air Base in Afghanistan. British troops were also

found to have mistreated prisoners and there were cases of prisoners dying in captivity. The stories caused international outrage and did immense harm to the image of the Coalition forces in Iraq and Afghanistan.

US Army guards escort a detainee at Camp X-ray in Guantánamo Bay, Cuba. An estimated 700 individuals have been detained at the Guantánamo Bay complex since 2001.

Extraordinary rendition

According to some human rights groups, the CIA had been involved in a practice known as "extraordinary rendition." This is the illegal moving of detainees to prisons in other countries. It was suggested that this was done so that detainees could be tortured by foreign agents, something prohibited under US law. Within days of taking office, President Obama ended this practice.

The fate of al-Qaeda

The invasion of Afghanistan certainly took the war to al-Qaeda, destroying its bases in Afghanistan and disrupting its activities. By the end of 2004, the US government declared it had killed or captured two thirds of the group's top figures. However, because of al-Qaeda's highly dispersed structure, with groups or cells in many different countries operating virtually independently of one another, the terrorist organization was able to survive. Also, Osama bin Laden remained uncaptured—possibly having moved to Pakistan—and continued to broadcast morale-boosting videotapes to his supporters around the world.

Global jihad

Al-Qaeda cells, or Islamists inspired by al-Qaeda, carried out large-scale attacks in many parts of the world over the next few years:

● On October 12, 2002, a bomb attack on a major tourist center in Bali, Indonesia, killed 202.

FACT FILE

Training camps

Al-Qaeda is thought to have used about 120 training camps in Afghanistan and Pakistan. The 9/11 Commission estimated that around 20,000 individuals may have been trained there between 1996 and 2001.

Emergency workers remove a victim of the al-Qaeda bomb attack, which destroyed two nightclubs in the Kuta Beach tourist area on Indonesia's resort island of Bali in October 2002.

- On March 11, 2004, terrorists linked to al-Qaeda planted bombs on a train in Madrid's Atocha Station, killing 191.
- On July 7, 2005, British-born jihadis carried out a series of coordinated bombings on trains and buses in London, killing 56.
- On July 11, 2006, seven bombs planted in trains killed 209 in Mumbai, India.
- On November 26–29, 2008, Mumbai was again the target as Islamist terrorists killed 173 in a prolonged series of attacks.

In many of these attacks, al-Qaeda played no direct role; it provided only inspiration. A rudimentary network of support and the recruitment of relatively small numbers of people to training camps were sufficient to set large numbers of young Islamists around the world on a path of terror.

Public support

As the war in Afghanistan has continued, with little sign of progress against the Taliban insurgency, public support in the United States and UK has declined. The death toll among Coalition troops continues to rise, yet there is no end to the conflict in sight. The fact that Islamist terrorist attacks have continued despite the war leaves many people wondering how much difference it has made. In their fight against the Coalition forces, the Taliban know they cannot win in a conventional war, so they have adopted the classic strategies of guerrilla warfare, avoiding pitched battles and conducting rapid raids and ambushes with bombs and booby traps. Similarly, al-Qaeda cannot hope to overcome the Western powers by force of arms, but it can try to wear down its enemies with a protracted struggle.

Families grieve as the coffins of three soldiers killed in Afghanistan are driven through the streets of Wootton Bassett, UK.

VOICES

A long struggle

General Sir David Richards, chief of general staff of the British Army, said:
I believe that the UK will be committed to Afghanistan in some manner— development, governance, security sector reform—for the next 30 to 40 years.

The London Times, August 8, 2009

8 THE LEGACY

One thing was clear to everyone who experienced the terrible events of 9/11, whether at first hand or on television: They knew that they were witnessing events that would change the world, even if they weren't sure exactly what that change would be.

A long war?

The events of that day stunned many Americans who had always unquestionably believed that their nation was a force for good in the world. It made them and all the citizens of the Western world face the fact that they had enemies who wished their destruction. No longer was it possible for Western citizens to ignore or be indifferent to the anger of many young Muslims regarding the policies and interventions of their governments. Whether it is viewed as a clash of civilizations or as a bid for political power, 9/11 signaled the beginning of a struggle that many experts believe will be a long one.

In remembrance of the 9/11 attacks, this Tribute in Light, created by 88 searchlights, was installed next to the site of the WTC in 2002.

Remembering the past—planning the future

New York had never experienced an attack on the scale of 9/11, and the initial mood of the city was one of shock. But like people in other cities around the world who have been bombed, New Yorkers soon demonstrated the strength of the human spirit in their own, unique style.

In place of the Twin Towers, a new complex, including 2.6 million square feet (241,000 square meters) of office space, an observation deck, and restaurant, has been planned. One World Trade Center, nicknamed Freedom Tower, will have 109 floors and reach the same height as the Twin Towers. It will be crowned by an antenna, which will take it to 1,776 feet (541 meters). The name and height are symbolic: "One World Trade Center" signals a desire to end conflict—for there to be "one world." The overall height of 1,776 feet recalls the date of the US Declaration of Independence and the belief in the rights of all men to be free and equal.

The complex will also contain a memorial and museum, with two reflecting pools marking the sites of the Twin Towers—a place in history that will not be forgotten.

FACT FILE

Freedom Tower

Work on the Freedom Tower began in 2006 and should be completed by 2013. The new tower will start as a cube and then turn into a square antiprism consisting of eight isosceles triangles.

An artist's impression of the Freedom Tower, designed by architects David Childs and Daniel Libeskind, which will be built on the site of the former World Trade Center.

GLOSSARY

adultery Voluntary sexual intercourse between a married person and a person who is not his or her spouse.

antiprism A complex geometric shape made up of triangular surfaces.

caliphate A united Muslim empire under the authority of a caliph.

CIA Central Intelligence Agency, a bureau responsible for intelligence and counterintelligence activies outside the United States.

coalition An alliance of countries working and fighting together for a common purpose.

Congress The national legislative body of the United States, consisting of the House of Representatives and the Senate.

dispersed Distributed or scattered.

fatwa A formal religious ruling issued by an Islamic leader.

FBI Federal Bureau of Investigation, a department of the US Department of Justice that deals with matters of national security and crimes against the government.

guerrilla A soldier who is not part of a regular army and fights by ambush and hit-and-run attacks.

insurgency A revolt against the government of a country.

Islamist Someone who follows a strict form of Islam based on a literal interpretation of the Qur'an and other holy Islamic scriptures.

isosceles triangle A triangle having two sides of equal length.

jihad The struggle for Islam. This can be interpreted either as a holy war, or as a spiritual striving.

mujahidin Muslim guerrilla fighters, especially in Afghanistan.

9/11 Commission A group established to investigate and produce a report on the events leading up to the 9/11 attacks.

Northern Alliance A multiethnic alliance of groups in Afghanistan who are united in their opposition to the Taliban.

Pentagon Headquarters of the US Department of Defense in Washington, D.C.

preemptive Intended to preempt or forestall something, such as to prevent an attack by disabling the enemy.

Sharia law Muslim religious law based on the teachings of the Islamic holy book, the Qur'an.

Shia The second largest branch of Islam, which considers Ali, a relative of Muhammad, and his descendents to be Muhammad's true successors.

Soviet Union Officially the Union of Soviet Socialist Republics (USSR), a communist-ruled federation of 15 republics, dominated by Russia, which lasted from 1922 to 1991.

Sunni The largest branch of Islam—90 percent of all Muslims are Sunni. They follow the teachings handed down by the first caliphs, successors of the Prophet Mohammed.

Taliban An Islamist political movement in Afghanistan.

terrorist Someone who uses violence to achieve political ends.

ultimatum A final demand or proposal, which if rejected will lead to war.

United Nations (UN) An organization representing the world's nations that tries to resolve international crises and promote world peace.

United Nations Security Council A group within the United Nations responsible for maintaining international peace and security. There are five permanent members (China, Russia, United States, UK, and France) and ten other members are elected to serve every two years.

weapons of mass destruction (WMD) Chemical, biological, or nuclear weapons capable of inflicting great loss of life.

White House The official residence of the president of the United States.

FURTHER INFORMATION

BOOKS

American Disasters: Attack on America: The Day the Twin Towers Collapsed by Mary Gow (Enslow Publishers, 2002)

Days that Changed the World: The September 11th Terrorist Attacks by Fiona MacDonald (World Almanac Library, 2003)

Global Questions: Can the War on Terrorism Be Won? by Alison Jamieson (Franklin Watts, 2008)

Secret History: The War on Terror by Brian Williams (Franklin Watts, 2010)

Snapshots in History: September 11: Attack on America by Andrew Langley (Compass Point Books, 2006)

Witness to History: September 11, 2001 by Sean Connolly (Heinemann Library, 2004)

WEBSITES

www.bbc.co.uk/religion/rcligions/islam
A BBC website introducing Islam.

dsc.discovery.com/convergence/twintowers/twintowers.html
Inside the Twin Towers: facts and statistics about the buildings.

http://edition.cnn.com/SPECIALS/2002/america.remembers
The CNN special edition covering all aspects of the 9/11 attacks and their legacy.

www.internet-esq.com/worldtradecenter/index.htm
Robert Swanson's memories and his gallery of photographs taken on 11 September 2001 in New York City.

www.9-11commission.gov
National Commission on Terrorist Attacks Upon the United States: includes downloads of the 9/11 Commission Report and the Executive Summary.

INDEX

Page numbers in **bold** refer to pictures.